Little Mitchie

Do Ants Sleep?

Do You Ever Wonder About Animals?

KIM THOMPSON

CREATING YOUNG NONFICTION READERS

Little Mitchie books spark curiosity and support early nonfiction reading for students in Grades 2-3. Designed to build vocabulary, support second language learners, and prepare readers for middle-grade content, each book includes helpful tips for parents and educators to build confidence and deepen understanding of the world.

TIPS FOR READING NONFICTION WITH BEGINNING READERS

Talk about Nonfiction

Begin by explaining that nonfiction books give us information that is true. The book will be organized around a specific topic or idea, and we may learn new facts through reading.

Look at the Parts

Most nonfiction books have helpful features. Our *Little Mitchie* titles include color photographs and graphic aids, a table of contents, a glossary, and an index. Share the purpose of these features with your reader.

Color Photos and Graphic Aids

A lot of information can be found by "reading" photos, charts, maps, and other graphic aids found within nonfiction texts. Help your reader learn more about the different ways information can be displayed.

Table of Contents

Located at the front of the book, this list shows the big ideas within the text and the page numbers where they can be found.

Glossary

Located at the back of the book, the glossary defines key words and phrases that are related to the topic. These words and phrases can be found in the text in colored type.

Index

Located at the back of the book, an index is an alphabetical list of topics and the page numbers where they can be found.

With a little help and guidance about reading nonfiction, you can feel good about introducing a young reader to the world of *Little Mitchie* nonfiction books.

Little Mitchie is an imprint of:

Mitchell Lane
PUBLISHERS

2001 SW 31st Avenue
Hallandale, FL 33009
mitchelllanepub.com

First Edition, 2027.

Author: Kim Thompson
Designer: Jen Bowers

Library of Congress Cataloging-in-Publication Data
Title: Do Ants Sleep? / by Kim Thompson

Description: Hallandale, FL :
Mitchell Lane Publishers, [2027]

Identifiers:
ISBN 979-8-89260-921-0 (library bound)
ISBN 979-8-89260-976-0 (eBook)

Library of Congress Control Number: 2026936393

PHOTO CREDITS
Shutterstock: cover, p.1 ©2025 Pawich Sattalerd, p.5 ©2016 NOPPHARAT236, p.6–7 ©2010 Sam DCruz, p.9 ©2018 frank60, p.10 ©2017 Poravute Siriphiroon, p.11 ©2015 Sanimfocus, p.13 ©2025 Kasturi2001, p.14 ©2026 Link42, p.17 ©2020 Erik Agar, p.18–19 ©2018 Jay Ondreicka, p.20 ©2012 Paulrommer SL, p.21 ©2010 Eric Isselee, p.22 ©Macrovector

TABLE OF CONTENTS

Chapter One

QUESTIONS

Have you ever watched ants **scurry** around? Were they exploring, carrying food, or rushing to and from their nest?

You probably wondered about the **insects**. You may have asked these questions.

1. Why are ants so busy?
2. Where are ants going in such a hurry?
3. Do ants ever sleep?

Chapter Two

WORKING TOGETHER

Ants live in **colonies**. Some build **anthills**. Some make nests underground or in trees.

ANIMAL WONDER
Big colonies can have over a million ants!

All colonies are busy. The ants work together to help the colony survive.

Queen ants lay eggs. **Drones** are male ants. They mate with the queen.

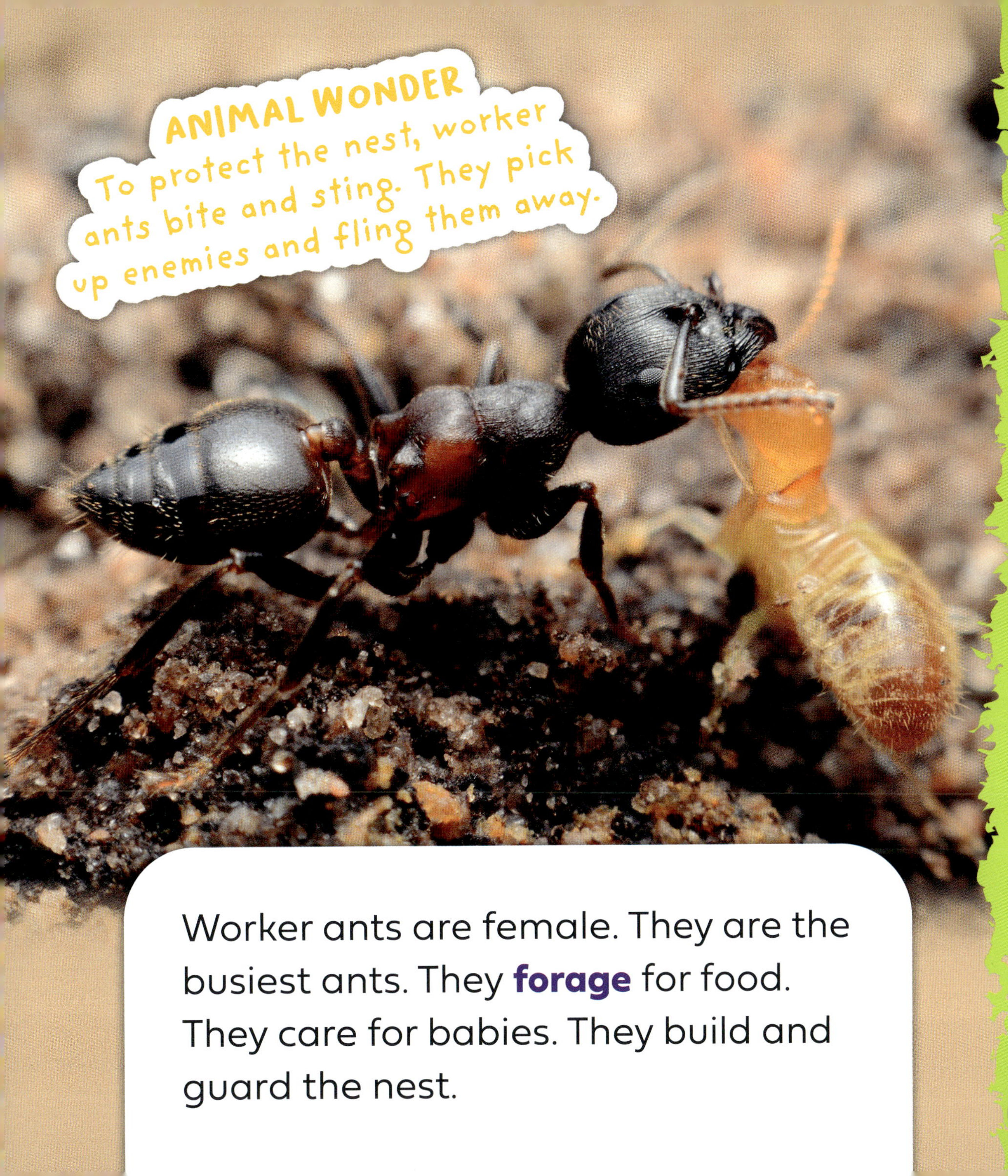

Worker ants are female. They are the busiest ants. They **forage** for food. They care for babies. They build and guard the nest.

Chapter Three

FOLLOWING A TRAIL

To work together, ants **communicate**. They talk to each other by producing chemicals called **pheromones**. An ant uses its **antennae** to sense pheromones.

ANIMAL WONDER

Ants travel as far as 650 feet (200 meters) away from their nests to find food. The position of the sun helps them know where they are.

Workers make pheromone trails that lead to food sources. Other workers follow the trails. They carry food home. They add more pheromones to make the best trails stronger.

Chapter Four

TAKING A SHORT BREAK

Worker ants have never-ending jobs. They can't afford to rest for very long. Of every ten workers, eight must be awake and active at all times.

Worker ants have **polyphasic** sleep. That means they sleep in short bursts. In 24 hours, a worker takes about 250 naps. Each nap lasts about one minute. That adds up to about four hours per day.

ANIMAL WONDER

Queen ants sleep about nine hours each day. They live much longer than workers. More sleep may be one reason.

Chapter Five

ANSWERS

Now, you can answer your questions.

1. **WHY ARE ANTS SO BUSY?**

   Ants work together to help the colony survive.

2. **WHERE ARE ANTS GOING IN SUCH A HURRY?**

   Worker ants make and follow chemical trails to find food.

3. **DO ANTS EVER SLEEP?**

   Yes, but worker ants are so busy that they sleep only in short bursts.

ANIMAL WONDER

Keep asking questions about animals. That's how you learn about the amazing creatures that share our world!

ANT DIAGRAM

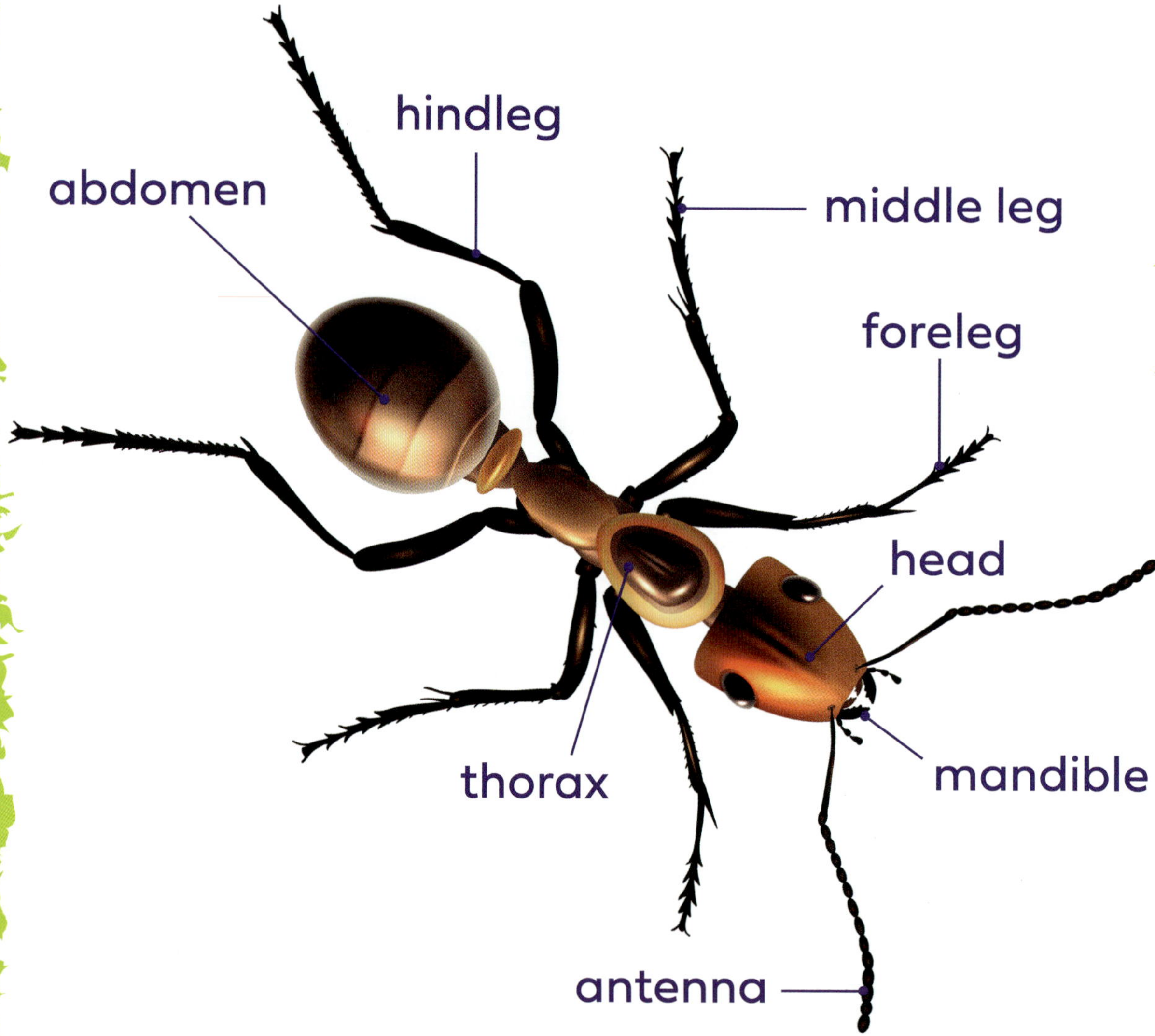
hindleg
abdomen
middle leg
foreleg
head
thorax
mandible
antenna

GLOSSARY

antennae (an-TEN-ee) pairs of sensory organs on the heads of insects

anthills (ANT-hilz) mounds of dirt that rise as ants dig their nests

colonies (KAH-luh-nees) large groups of animals that live together

communicate (kuh-MYOO-ni-kate) to share information and feelings

drones (drohnz) male ants that have wings and whose function is to mate with the queen

forage (FOR-ij) to search for food

insects (IN-sekts) small animals that have hard outer skeletons instead of backbones and that have three pairs of legs and three body sections

pheromones (FAIR-uh-mones) chemical substances produced by animals to provide warnings, attract mates, or give information

polyphasic (pah-lee-FAY-zic) made up of many periods, or phases

scurry (SKUR-ee) to move with light, quick steps; to hurry

FURTHER READING

Bittel, Jason. *How to Talk to a Tiger. . .And Other Animals: How Critters Communicate in the Wild.* Harry N. Abrams, 2021.

Gerdeman, Beverly. *Ants for Kids: A Junior Scientist's Guide to Queens, Drones, and the Hidden World of Ants.* Callisto Kids, 2021.

ON THE INTERNET

FactFactory Lab: Surprising Truths about One of Nature's Hardest Workers
youtube.com/watch?v=LByye66o1EQ
Watch ants as they work together in amazing ways.

National Geographic Kids: 10 Cool Facts about Ants!
natgeokids.com/uk/discover/animals/insects/ant-facts
Discover amazing facts about these busy insects.

SciShow Kids: How Do Ants Find Food?
youtube.com/watch?v=2IVb2Atu3Jc
Learn more about how ants work together to feed the colony.

INDEX